Made in the USA
Middletown, DE
02 May 2022

65118010R00057